The International Journal
of Sports & Ethics

The International Journal
of Sports & Ethics

authorHOUSE®

AuthorHouse™
1663 Liberty Drive
Bloomington, IN 47403
www.authorhouse.com
Phone: 1-800-839-8640

First published by AuthorHouse   05/17/2011

ISBN: 978-1-4567-6532-3 (sc)
ISBN: 978-1-4567-6531-6 (ebk)

Printed in the United States of America

Any people depicted in stock imagery provided by Thinkstock are models, and such images are being used for illustrative purposes only.
Certain stock imagery © Thinkstock.

This book is printed on acid-free paper.

Because of the dynamic nature of the Internet, any web addresses or links contained in this book may have changed since publication and may no longer be valid. The views expressed in this work are solely those of the author and do not necessarily reflect the views of the publisher, and the publisher hereby disclaims any responsibility for them.

International Sports Professionals Association:

25 East Washington Street Suite 1615
Chicago, IL 60602
312-920-9522
www.theISPA.org

Contents

Address From Editor

The International Sports Professionals Association would like to welcome you to the first edition of *The ISPA Journal of Sports and Ethics*. We are very excited to share with you this wealth of knowledge from our Credentialed Professionals. You will find this journal to be an exciting blend of articles based on research, qualitative method and commentary. ISPA always prides itself on being a trendsetter and the ISPA Journal is no exception. Nowhere will you find a journal with such diversity. Throughout these pages both the expertise and passion of our Credentialed Professionals will be evident. As always we welcome your comments, as it is our mission to make the ISPA Journal amongst the very best.

Yours in Sport,
Justin Mayer
Chief Editor-ISPA Journal of Sports & Ethics
JMayer@theISPA.org

Editors Note:

From May 23rd to July 25th we will be accepting submissions for the second issue of *The ISPA Journal of Sports and Ethics*. Please see guidelines for submission below.

- 1500-3000 Words
- Sports Related content
- Citations follow APA standards
- Contains brief bio about yourself

SPORTS ETHICS

The Ethical Sports Psychologist

By Andrea Corn Ph. D.

Over the past decade the field of Sports psychology has become popularized, at times glamorized, but overall, increasingly more specialized and diverse. Today's field draws from an interdisciplinary group of professionals including psychologists, clinical sport and exercise psychologists, physical educators, behavioral scientists, athletic trainers, sports physicians, nutritionists plus a variety of other allied professionals. For those who work in the capacity as a sport psychologist or as a sports psychology consultant our job is to apply and integrate psychological theories, the latest research, and sometimes draw upon personal experiences to provide psychological services to athletes of all ages and abilities.

In some cases, sport psychologists have the good fortune to treat individuals who are not only highly talented, motivated, and high achieving but also relatively strong mentally, physically, and emotionally. Of course, this is not always the case, as no athlete or individual goes through life unscathed. Even gifted and talented athletes will seek out therapeutic services for a myriad of reasons, such as emotional disorders (including mood or anxiety disorders, anorexia, or substance abuse), as well as mental or physical difficulties following injuries, burnout, unable to concentrate, or how to cope with problems outside the world of sports but nonetheless, are affecting the athlete's personal, family life, or intimate relationships. However, this paper is going to focus on a narrow topic and discusses the importance of maintaining healthy and appropriate boundaries working with athletes.

MENTAL AND EMOTIONAL TRAINING

Generally speaking, highly competitive athletes seek out a sport psychologist to align mind and body in the quest of pursuing greater success, achieving excellence, or to overcome unrealistic and self-defeating ideas. If the athlete has already attained a modicum of success it informs the sport psychologist that the athlete has the raw talent and emotional and mental skills to potentially rise and reach his or her optimal performance.

RELATIONSHIP BOUNDARIES

While an athlete is free to share his or her successes (as well as disappointments) freely with others, the sport psychologist or consultant cannot. It may be tempting to want to bask in the same positive light and recognition the athlete receives, but that is not our role. Despite whatever gratification is derived working with athletes, our sense of purpose, duty, and satisfaction in our role must be contained and metaphorically held inside ourselves. Therapeutically, any personal feelings of pride and accomplishment must come from the knowing each one of us did our best in working with the athlete.

Some athletes will be able to acknowledge progress, or realize the benefits of making constructive changes, and the insight subsequently attained. Of course, this doesn't always occur, even if the sports psychologists' best efforts were given. There will be those athletes who do not appreciate or understand how important the therapeutic relationship is in creating a new way of seeing oneself. Or, some athletes despite repeated statements about seeking self-improvement, end up unwilling to change familiar ways of behaving (even if self-destructive or self-defeating).

What really stands out is the fact that an athlete's feats as well as blunders are readily accessible and can travel instantaneously, whether through the Internet, virtual sports pages, websites, twitter accounts, or shared on social media sites. As much as some athletes welcome the local to global recognition, when events go badly, it leaves them with few places to hide. And, coupled with poor decision an athlete's words and actions can boomerang very quickly raising bigger concerns about his or her maturity and discretion. For example, this summer we witnessed a situation with NBA star Michael Beasly, formerly of the Miami Heat; now playing with the Toronto Raptor. Following an unusual, eye-catching Twitter photo this NBA athlete's posting was carefully scrutinized. Shortly thereafter, he wound up entering a rehab facility due to violating the NBA's substance abuse policy. As professionals we may wonder why any professional athlete might be willing to be so transparent and reveal thoughts or feelings that could pose a risk to his or her career. Not knowing any more than what has already been reported in the news, I wish to turn the spotlight back to our own profession, as there is an important lesson and cautionary tale to consider.

WAYS TO ACHIEVE PROFESSIONAL RECOGNTION

As a psychologist or sports psychologist, our measuring stick of achievement is best witnessed through increased referrals, seeing new patients come to our offices through word of mouth, positive feedback or recommendations from colleagues or friends. Additional ways to receive external recognition can occur through professional involvements in other organizations, such as the APA, (Division 47, Exercise and Sport Psychology), AASP (Association of Applied Sports Psychology, which has its own Ethics Code), and the newly formed ISPA (International Society Professionals Association). Other means include teaching and educating students; whether at the collegiate or graduate level, writing articles, chapters in textbook, journals, or other professional publications. Personal gratification and success can also occur by sharing one's experience, wisdom and knowledge at conferences, seminars, or in supervision. Regardless, our role is to protect our patient's well being, safeguard their privacy, and uphold the principles and ethical guidelines of our profession. If not, than the psychologist needs to first ask him or herself why . . . because something must be lacking or is out of conscious awareness but leads this individual to blur or at worst, cross this invisible boundary line.

Following an APA conference in 2005, Stephen Behnke was quoted as saying,

"The goal is for our members and the profession to view ethics not as a set of external constraints that limit our possibilities and inhibit our creativity, but rather as a part of the fabric of our professional lives, and ethical dilemmas not as a sign that something has gone wrong in our work, but rather as reflecting the richness, complexity, and importance of what psychologists do"

Thus it strongly recommended to any sport psychologist or consult to reacquaint oneself and reread the APA Ethics Code, which is comprised of an Introduction, a Preamble, five General Principles, and Ethical Standards. The Preamble and General Principles are inspirational goals pointing to the highest ideals within our profession. Even though this section of the code is rarely enforced, it underscores the right course of action. Even AASP has adopted the APA's Ethic Code but have tailored them so they uphold the values and mission of this sports organization. Given the limited space of this article, I will list the sections as a reminder of the spectrum of material covered (See below).

Everyone of us has our own moral and ethical compass that guides us in our work with the talented athletes that we treat. And, regardless of the athlete's physical and God-given talents, working out mind-body problems occur within the sanctity and privacy of the therapeutic space or office (Sometimes this space has to be portable to accommodate an athlete's schedule). And, while each athlete's accomplishments and achievements are visibly and public for the world to see; those of us who work therapeutically with athletes, the opposite must be true. Here, our work must be done privately, with complete confidentiality and respect for this individual, his or her issues, and course of treatment. Some cases will be challenging, and if the psychologist feels ill equipped to handle the problem, then he or she needs to seek out additional supervision and guidance. At the same time, the psychologist would benefit from re-reading the APA's and/or AASP's Ethic Code of Conduct.

Preamble and General Principles:

Principle A: Beneficence and Nonmaleficence
Principle B: Fidelity and Responsibility
Principle C: Integrity
Principle D: Justice
Principle E: Respect for People's Rights and Dignity
Standard 1: Resolving Ethical Issues
Standard 2: Competence
Standard 3: Human Relations
Standard 4: Privacy and Confidentiality
Standard 5: Advertising and Other Public Statement
Standard 6: Record Keeping and Fees
Standard 7: Education and Training
Standard 8: Research and Publication
Standard 9: Assessment
Standard 10: Therapy

In closing, ask yourself, when was the last time you looked at the APA or AASP Ethical Guidelines? If you have a hard time remembering when it was, then it may be worth the time and effort so you cause emotional or mental harm to your patient or yourself as well as risk the repercussions that would be imposed on you by our fine profession.

About the Author:

Dr. Andrea Corn is a sports psychology consultant in private practice in Lighthouse Point, FL, where she sees children, adolescents, and adults. She is also a highly regarded psychologist in the area of child and adolescent development, youth sports, and family matters. Dr. Corn has spoken locally as well as nationally at conferences on youth sport issues. She is a member of the American Psychological Association (APA), including the Division of Exercise and Sport Psychology (47), the Association of Applied Sport Psychology (AASP) and the International Sports Professionals Association (ISPA).

Dr. Corn has written articles on various sports related topics for The National Alliance of Youth Sports (NAYS), South Florida Parenting, and The Miami Herald. Dr. Corn taught Sport Psychology at St. Thomas University in Miami to undergraduate and graduate students. For several years, Dr. Corn served on AASP's Committee for Child and Adolescent Sport Related Issues and has written several of their position papers on youth sports.

References

Behnke, S. (2005, November). Ethics at APA's Annual Convention. *Monitor on Psychology, pp. 74-75*

Maximizing Your Effectiveness with Young Athletes: A Developmental Perspective

By John E. Mayer, Ph.D.

Guiding young athletes is a complex endeavor. Coaches, volunteers, and professionals in all fields of sports become frustrated when trying to lead young people. The problem is an age old one when adults attempt to apply a successful method used on adults and assuming that these same methods will work just as successfully on young people. I addressed this issue early in my career when I called attention to the special needs of teenagers and substance abuse. Young people's needs in substance abuse detection and treatment were not being met because professionals applied the successful techniques from adult alcohol and substance abuse field and assumed that these techniques would work just as well on youth. The problem was that these successful techniques were not built upon the developmental needs and capacities of youth. Thus, not only couldn't young people relate to these techniques, they did not meet their specific needs.

The field of sports finds itself in this same position. A large part of the dilemma for sports professionals is that young people have changed in their attitudes and abilities significantly in the last sixty years yet sports approaches young people as if they are still in the mid 1900s. Young people are increasingly being turned off by adults leading them in sports because they just can't relate to techniques used to guide them. Again, this phenomenon of leadership is not unique to sports. Many professional fields employ techniques that I would term, 'revolving-door' techniques. For example, it is well known in medicine that physicians employ techniques that they learned in residency then teach these techniques to new physicians and so forth and so on. My book, *Family Fit*, chronicled how many of our favorite eating habits have their origins from a society that was agriculturally based. People's lives were dominated by manual labor and physical activity thus they required higher caloric needs. Change is slow.

The problem in sports is not with the X's and O's. The techniques of playing sports have evolved tremendously. The problem lies with the leadership of young people with leadership techniques that have no grounding in the developmental stages of youth.

Let's review what we know about child/adolescent development and offer suggestions on how these techniques can be applied to sports success. Let s also assume that our young athletes begin to participate in sports at 5 years old. This is a convenient starting age because the considerations for adult leadership are the same for younger athletes prior to this entry age who may be participating in sports.

Ages 5 to 7

From age 5 to 7, children are very heavily into the 'Me' stage of overall development. The concept of peers or others in the world is a vague one at best. Children are building skills at this age to reconcile the world around them by understanding that people and things can be dependable and trusted. They are also just learning how to control impulses and to obey rules and live with an internal sense of order and regularity. Cognitively they struggle still with connecting their behavior with consequences, so when parents discipline children at this age it is hard for the child to 'generalize' consequences to other behaviors. This is frustrating for parents.

In sports, consider these same dynamics, as parents should. Young athletes at this age will impulsively leave the field of play or court and do what they feel like. This action is not rebellion, this is being a child. Don't treat it as defiance. Firmly and respectfully guide the child back to the task at hard. Remember at this age patience on their part is very weak. Keep practices and even games short and very, very concrete. Children at this age are not 'stringing' directions (game plays, rules, techniques) together to establish a system. They can best follow minute, careful, circumscribed directions to elicit the desired actions. Keep the field of play small, and then there will be less chance for distraction and departure from the game. Young athletes at this age are highly distracted.

Ages 7 to 11

From age 7 to 11, young people begin to be aware of their peers more and develop increasing consideration of the feelings and needs of their peers. Further, the importance of peer relationships begins to have more significance. They are moving away from the influence of their parents and the adults around them as the only consequence on their life and actions. The beginnings of bullying and teasing behaviors are seen more as the opinions of others are now more important. 5th and 6th grade in school is a heightened time to witness bullying and teasing. Cognitively although they are still in a stage where concrete thinking dominates, they increasingly obtain the ability to string or chain experiences together. They can maintain the rules of games and follow-through with rules and structure. People, objects, rules, and structure gain permanence to them. They trust more and are better able to control their impulses. They can respond to consequences more. But these consequences have to be immediate and be specific to them.

In sports, techniques such as, "If you don't behave at practice you won't start on Saturday." Just don't have an effect. Such consequences are simply too far into the future. Similarly, giving them profound statements about doing things for the good of the team, etc., are wasted. Athletes at this age are still in the 'Me' stage of social relations. Coaches are often tricked at this age by a young athlete's abilities because parents typically get more involved in their child's sports. For example, a coach may use a future orientated technique and think it works but what is really happening is that the parent is constantly reminding and maybe brow-beating the child at home about the consequence, so it is staying uppermost in the child's mind. So, the coach is actually training the parent(s) more than the young athlete. The sport has to continue to be fun and have positive value for the child for them to maintain interest and enthusiasm. The theme for them is: What have you done for me lately?

Age 12 to 14

From age 12 to 14, peers become even more important, but parents still maintain the dominant influence on young people. Young people this age are still in 'right and wrong' black and white methods of thinking about the world or as Piaget called the cognitive stage of concrete operations. Interest and activity directed to the opposite sex takes a center stage at this age. One of the first migrations away from sports participation occurs as other life distractions arrive in the child's awareness. Along with attraction to the opposite sex, there are video games, cell phones, texting, FaceBook, music, all kinds of social goodies that take interest away from sports. Failure becomes another fuel for migration away from sports. Often prior to this age the inability to perform in sports was not a perceived deficit in the young athlete. The recognition of failure is both a cognitive development and a nuance of sports in society. Prior to age 12, kids play sports with this same narcissistic or 'Me' outlook. Now, at this age, they can perceive how others perform, they can realize how they stack up against other players on their team because social awareness is building and becoming more acute. The young athlete is increasingly measuring themselves against others. This social judgment may result in frustration, sadness, and withdrawal in the young athlete. The result is that they want to quit. It is still important at this age to emphasize the individual rewards for sports participation.

Age 15 to 17

From age 15 to 17, social life expands even greater. Dating, driving, more liberal recreation hours, and other adult-like privileges expand. Thinking about the true feelings of others and developing empathy and concern for social good is now developing. The young person is actively moving away from a 'Me' orientation to think and empathize with the feelings and needs others. The good of the team now has more meaning. Techniques that emphasize the good of the whole group have some power in the teenager's life. But, these adult-like temptations are very powerful as well and one of the largest migrations away from sports participation occurs during this age group. The good news here is that those players that stay with their sport are typically those who have the most commitment and internal motivation.

A special note on teenage development is extremely important to consider. Teenage maturity is very unpredictable. Some teens will develop faster than others and visa versa. So, the paradox for some adults leading teens in sports is that some of the techniques they employ that are not age appropriate may be effective on the teens they are guiding because they are precocious and their cognitive growth can absorb and thrive under them. So, a common dilemma of adults is the observation that some of my players "get it", but the majority don't. What's going on? What's going on is that they are teens and teenage maturity is not uniform across any group of adolescents participating in any activity, let alone sports.

The guidelines set down here apply to the majority of teens. Another factor to consider in the precariousness of teenage development is intellectual capabilities. Those teenagers of higher intellectual capacity generally will mature faster than those of more limited intellectual ability. Adults who lead teens in sports must understand this wide discrepancy in the abilities across typical teenagers.

Age 18 to 22

For the majority of young adults in this age range their cognitive and social development has advanced such that they are fully into the 'We' stage of social cognition. Young people this age thrive on thinking about the good of the group and the by-products of group efforts. Teamwork and sportsmanship are idealized and embraced. This is not to say that certain players won't be selfish and narcissistic, but these will be expressions of their own personality deficits and not necessarily by-products of their developmental stage.

Importantly now during this period the young person can fully appreciate and look forward to the future. Prior to this age young people were largely concerned with the here and now. It is very difficult to motivate younger athletes to look at the long-term benefits of their efforts. Now, future rewards are understandable, even desirable for the athlete at this age.

Most of us are aware that it is at this age when the young person is beginning to consider their place in society and to contemplate, even plan their role as an adult. This is the well-known quest for identity. Being an athlete is very soothing to this quest. Athletics give the young person meaning and purpose. It is for this reason why ancient methods of negative reinforcement, insults, and punitive techniques are particularly harmful to the athlete at this age. Identity builds more successfully by positive reinforcement of the self-concept that the young athlete is building. Sure, some athletes may show a positive response to the primitive methods of decades past, but I would maintain to you that these reactions are a result of the response to competitiveness and not the motivation to the individual's personality. The problem with these negative motivational styles is that they are very short lived for the athlete. The athlete will respond for short bursts of performance under these techniques, but over the long haul (Or a full season) the athlete will fail. This is because of the cognitive and social maturity of the athlete at this age. There are effective methods of motivating young athletes at this age and at all the ages discussed in this article. Let's examine these techniques. But, first let's consider effective techniques for communicating (talking) to young people based on the developmental knowledge outlined above. Then, we will discuss motivating young people in a more effective manner.

Special Tips for Communicating with Young Athletes:

- **Establish respect.** Kids know you are an adult, don't try to be a buddy or the cool dude coach. Kids have tremendous Lie Dar and will see right through communication techniques that try to be anything other than who you are as an adult and a leader for them.
- **Listen.** I mean really listen. Take an interest in their lives. Remember that the things that are important in their lives might not seem like such a big deal to you, but for them these things are nuclear bombs exploding all around them. Put yourself in their shoes-don't look at their life like an adult. Picture life as it presents itself to them. Remember so many things they are experiencing are for the first time and they are not going to perform them as YOU would.
- **Watch you body language.** Don't do goofy actions such as squatting down to their level or patting them on the head, etc. Again, they know you are an adult, bigger than they and you don't talk with kid slang or baby talk. Always make eye contact and talk directly to them not ABOUT them in front of the other adults.

- Model communication. Children and young people learn best by seeing how you communicate to others. Talk to all those around you in the same respectful, empathic way you want them to talk to you. No yelling, abusive language or expletives. No teasing, no sarcasm, don't lose your temper.
- **Empower young people.** Make their ideas and opinions worthy by taking them into consideration. No question is a bad question. Seek out their advice. It is great for them to hear, "What do you think we should do in this situation?"
- **Be patient.** Young people are not finished products; many communication skills are things they just haven't learned yet. This doesn't make them unsocialized, disadvantaged, or deficient, it makes them KIDS. Don't expect young people to be perfect or to do things how you would.

Special Tips on Motivating Young People:

- **Attitude-Attitude-Attitude.** Motivating children and youth starts with the attitude you present to them. Your attitude should be one of kindness and teaching. You are giving something to the kids. Your attitude should convey this service orientation. Be positive, supply the energy in the relationship with the child.
- **Surround the young people with Motivation.** Use positive affirmations liberally and often. A good resource for these are the affirmations researched from the *Search Institute* in Minnesota. They call these affirmations: *The 40 Developmental Assets.* These 40 assets are social actions that this foundation's research has shown are important in the healthy development of a child/youth. Take a look at these are they can be valuable references of ways you can approach a child with affirmations.
- **The best motivator of all is verbal praise from an adult.** Verbal praise given face-to-face by an adult beats other motivators such as money, gifts, material rewards of all types and even peer accolades. Use verbal praise liberally with young people.
- **Praise effort and not accomplishment.** Affirming the effort a young person puts into an athletic endeavor is more motivating than affirming the accomplishment. Accomplishment is the result of so many intangible and tangible factors that are not in the sole control of the child-the competitor's skills and resources, a lucky bounce, mistakes, bad calls, etc.—so the effort a young person puts into an athletic activity is so much more ripe for motivation than the accomplishment. Further, accomplishment is often translated by the young person as praise for their native ability or potential and this ability/potential can be transitory. When you praise effort in this way, you are emphasizing skill development over results and you will see huge growth in the young athlete from this emphasis.
- **Don't crush them over mistakes.** Use mistakes as the ultimate teaching moment. It is commonly acknowledged that we earn best from our mistakes. Capitalize on these opportunities for the child to learn.
- **Don't confuse the lack of motivation from the lack of ability.** Assess the youth's abilities honestly and motivate with all the concepts listed here within their abilities. This is where praising effort is so important. You are motivating the less capable athlete with praise even tough the results of their efforts are not accomplishing as much as the more talented athlete.

- **<u>Sarcasm and negative motivation has no place in the leadership of today's young athletes.</u>** That says it all.
- **<u>Internal Motivators are more powerful than External Motivators.</u>** Many adults believe that by being dominant over the young athlete, they will perform better. Fear techniques, yelling, berating the young athlete, aggressive techniques are all examples of external motivators. These motivators are seductive. They can appear to work effectively temporarily especially while the adult leader is present to apply the external motivation. But, they are transitory because take the external motivator away and the young athlete quickly becomes unmotivated, even subversive. It is important to note here that for the athletes at The youngest ages as listed here (5-7 and 7-11) external motivators and motivations do work better than the internal centered. This is because the cognitive and social development of the child athlete at these ages is not advanced enough to develop internal motivation sufficiently. This occurs as a result of all the developmental conditions outlined in those sections above. Children at these ages love to play for play's sake, but to expect them to have an allegiance to the 'sport' is shortsighted. They are just being children who love to play.

In summary, the following principles will result in great leadership of young athletes.

Successful General Concepts that are effective across all ages of athletes:

- BE CONSISTENT
- BE RESPECTFUL
- ALWAYS IMPOSE BOUDARIES-STRUCTRURE-DISCIPLINE
- BE EMPATHIC
- COMMUNICATE EFFECTIVELY
- LISTEN
- USE AFFIRMATIONS
- SET HIGH STANDARDS BUT REALIZE THAT YOUNG PEOPLE WILL FAIL
- ALWAYS BE A MODEL AND A TEAM PLAYER YOURSELF
- LEAD THEM BASED ON THEIR DEVELOPMENTAL CAPABILITIES-NOT ON AN ADULT STANDARD BY WHICH YOU WERE LEAD.

About the Author:

Dr. John Mayer is a practicing Clinical Psychologist acclaimed for treating adolescents, children, families, violent and acting out patients, substance abusers and disorders of young adults. A native Chicagoan, he received his doctorate from Northwestern University Medical School. Dr. Mayer is the author of over 60 professional articles, most on family life, and 10 books. Dr. Mayer currently serves as the President of the International Sports Professionals Association. In addition to being an Author, Clinician and lecturer, Dr. Mayer is an avid triathlete and marathon runner.

References

Arsenio, W. F., Adams, E., & Gold, J. (2009). Social information processing, moral reasoning, and emotion attributions: Relations with adolescents' reactive and proactive aggression. *Child Development, 80, 1739-1755. doi:10.1111/j.1467-8624.2009.01365.x*

Arsenio, W. F., & Gold, J. (2006*).* The effects of social injustice and inequality on children's moral judgments and behavior: Towards a theoretical model. *Cognitive Development, 21, 388-400. doi:10.1016/j.cogdev.2006.06.005*

Bright-Paul, Alexandra; Jarrold, Christopher; Wright, Daniel B. (2008). *Developmental Psychology, Vol 44(4), Jul 2008, 1055-1068. doi: 10.1037/0012-1649.44.4.1055*

Davis, Douglas D. (2010). Child Development: A Practitioners Guide. *New York: Guilford. 494 pgs.*

Gräfenhain, M, Behne, T, Carpenter, M, Tomasello. (2009). Developmental Psychology. *Vol 45(5), Sep 2009, 1430-1443. doi: 10.1037/a0016122*

Kall, Robert V. Advances in Child Development and Behavior. *Vol.35 2010. New York: Elsevier*

Maholmes, Valerie, et. al. (2010) Applied Research in Child and Adolescent Development: A Practical Guide. *New York: Taylor & Francis. 340 pgs.*

Mayer, J and Filstead, W. (1984). Adolescence and Alcohol. *New York: Ballinger*

Mayer, J. (1989). The Adolescent Alcohol Involvement Scale-*AAIS.*

Mayer, J. (2009) Family Fit. *Chicago: NP2/ISPA Pub.*

Piaget, J. (1981). Intelligence and affectivity: Their relationship during child development *(T. Brown & C. Kaegi, Trans.). Palo Alto, CA: Annual Reviews.*

Posner, M, Rothbart, M. (2007). Educating the human brain. *Washington, DC, US: American Psychological Association. (2007). xiii, 263 pp. doi: 10.1037/11519-000*

Santrock, John M. (2010) Child Development. The 40 Developmental Assets. *New York: McGraw-Hill. 648 pgs. Search Institute Minneapolis, MN.*

SPORTS PERFORMANCE

Body Composition and its Affect on the Sports Performance Spectrum

By Dawn Weatherwax-Fall, RD, CSSD, LD, ATC, LAT, CSCS

Having a certain body fat to muscle mass ratio is related to athletic performance. Research has shown that correct portion of muscle mass increases strength, power, and agility (Spaniol, 2002) (Spaniol, 1997). Table 1 (see next page) provides recommend body fat percentages for both men and women. However, to gain lean muscle it is not just about the exercise protocol but nutritional intake and timing (Biolo, Williams, Fleming, & Wolfe, 1999) (Rasmussen, Tipton, Miller, Wolf, &Wolfe, 2000) Research shows three out of four student athletes may not be getting enough to eat. It also shows that 70% of the women and 73% of the men are not getting enough total calories, only 81% of the women and 90% of the men are consuming enough carbohydrates, and just 68% of the women and 81% of the men are eating enough protein based on USDA guidelines. Intakes of salt, total fat, saturated fat, and cholesterol often exceed recommendations, even in diets deficient in major components (Hinton, Sanford, Davidson, Yakushko, & Beck, 2004). To help you achieve your goals, you should know your body composition. But body composition is much more than a body fat percentage number. Below are different ways the measurement can be utilized.

1. Knowing what percent body fat assists in the type of fuel mixture an athlete needs. If an athlete has a higher body fat they usually need fewer calories and fewer carbohydrates. The opposite is true if the athlete has a low body fat. They usually need more calories and carbohydrates due to more lean weight.

2. In any strength and conditioning or specialized nutrition program there needs to be a way to measure its effectiveness. Body composition testing is an important measurement tool since most athletes want to gain muscle, lose fat, or do both.

3. When you are evaluating body fat percentages the challenge is not to just evaluate the percent body fat number but to also evaluate the lean weight number. Even though you may have the appropriate body fat percentage for your sport, you may still have room for improvement if you continue to gain lean mass.

4. When an athlete has encountered a severe injury where rehabilitation will take several months, measuring body composition on a monthly basis can be a tool to minimize a gain in body fat. Athletes can gain body fat quickly when activity has been limited and

eating habits are poor. It is difficult to get an athlete back to "full go" if they have lost muscle and gained body fat.

5. Body Composition testing can be a reassurance test. Many female athletes believe when they gain weight, they are gaining fat. Also an athlete can exchange fat at the same rate they gain muscle so the scale is not displaying the positive exchange.

6. Because female athletes are more vulnerable to developing an eating disorder (Kirk, Singh, & Getz, 2001) having biyearly body composition tests can detect any significant changes. These changes could shed light on an unhealthy behavior with food.

Classification	Women	Men
Essential	10 – 12%	2 – 4%
Athletes	14 – 20%	6 – 13%
Fitness	21 – 24%	14 – 17%
Acceptable	25 – 31%	18 – 25%
Plus	32% plus	25% plus

Table 1

The best ways to measure body composition are by hydrostatic weighing, Dexa Scan or Bod Pod testing. However many people do not have access or the funds to use these methods. The next best step is to use Lange skin fold calipers. They are easy to use, easy to learn, and very affordable. However you want to make sure you take the time and follow strict protocols to ensure accuracy (Heyward & Wagner, 2004). Take a minimum of three tests at each site and have at least two numbers that are within a millimeter. If you do not, then keep retesting the site until you do. The last thing you want is the body fat percentage to increase due to poor measuring techniques. Lastly you want to avoid going the easy route and buy a bioempedance device. These devices can be anywhere from 6-10% off because these techniques depend on the athletes hydration status (McArdle, Katch & Katch, 2006). These tools start off by measuring how fast the current runs through the body. The more hydrated the athlete the lower the body fat will register. The more dehydrated the athlete is the higher the body fat will measure. Body Composition testing is not just about measuring fat. It can be a very effective tool for menu planning, monitoring progress, improving current athletic status, part of a rehabilitation protocol, offering encouragement, and finding irregularities in behavior. Now that is a tool.

About the Author:

Dawn Weatherwax-Fall is a Registered/Licensed Dietitian with a specialty in Sports Nutrition and Founder of Sports Nutrition 2Go. She is also a Board Certified Specialist in Sports Dietetics. In addition, she is an Athletic Trainer with a Certification in Strength and Conditioning from The National Strength and Conditioning Association. Therefore, she brings a comprehensive and unique understanding of the athlete's body, and its nutritional needs, to those interested in achieving specific performance goals and optimal health. Weatherwax-Fall is also the author of The Official Snack Guide for Beleaguered Sports Parents and The Complete Idiot's Guide to Sports Nutrition. She is an Official Speaker for the Gatorade Sports Science Institute and on the approval speaker list for the NCAA. She has also been featured on television shows including: Good Morning America, MSNBC, Geraldo Rivera, and Fox News.

References

Lippincott Williams & Wilkins. (2005). ACSM's Guidelines for Exercise Testing Prescription. *American College of Sports Medicine (7th Edition). Philadelphia.*

Biolo, G, Williams, BD, Fleming, RY, and Wolfe, RR. (1999). Insulin action on muscle protein kinetics and amino acid transport during recovery after resistance exercise. *Diabetes, 48:949-957.*

Heyward, VH, Wagner, DR. (2004). Applied Body Composition Assessment. *Champaign, IL: Human Kinetics.*

Hinton, P, Sanford, T, Davidson, MM, Yakushko, O, and Beck, N. (2004). Nutrient intake and dietary behaviors of male and female collegiate athletes. *International Journal of Sports Nutrition and Exercise Metabolism, 14: 389-390.*

Kirk, G, Singh, K, and Getz H. (2001). Risk of Eating Disorders among female college athletes and non athletes. *Journal of College Counseling, 4(2): 122-132.*

McArdle, W, Katch, F, Katch, V. (2006). Exercise Physiology. (4th Edition). *Philadelphia: Lippincott Williams & Wilkins.*

Rasmussen B, Tipton, KD, Miller, SL, Wolf, SE, and Wolfe, RR. (2000). An oral essential amino acid carbohydrate supplement enhances muscle protein anabolism after resistance exercise. *Journal of Applied Physiology, 88:386-392.*

Spaniol FJ. Physiological predictors of bat speed and throwing velocity in adolescent Baseball players (Abstract). (2002). *Journal of Strength and Conditioning Research, 16(4): 1-18.*

Spaniol FJ. (1997). Predicting throwing velocity in college baseball players (Abstract). *Journal of Strength and Conditioning Research, 11(4): 286.*

The Competitive Mindset as Part of a Comprehensive Structure

By John C. Panepinto, M.Ed, LPC, CSC

In my youth I listened to baseball games on the radio and imagined what it was like to be like my hero, Mickey Mantle. In our one bedroom flat in the Bronx, I would huddle with the old Admiral transistor, glued to every pitch. I would look over my Topps Mantle card as he stepped up and hoped he'd blast one toward the façade in Yankee stadium . . .

I only got to see Mantle play once in person. He hit a mammoth shot that day, high and deep into the seats. I was young enough to think that he caused the skies to open up with that shot. The rains came and the game was called. The homer didn't count because the game hadn't reached the fifth inning. But, the homer counted to me.

As a youngster, I knew so little about Mickey Mantle. He was a hero to me regardless, because of what I imagined him to be, because of my innocence. He was the true archetype of a hero, the structure woven in our unconscious: strong, courageous in the face of adversity. Surely, he would never let me down.

We are not so innocent today. Today, technology has grown the capacity to view even the subtle nuances of athletic performances, and the media digs deeper for details after the event is long over. It seems as if little is left to imagination—or not? Despite technology and science, we do not have total access to the athlete's mindset as these processes are private, subjective and, in some part as psychotherapists can attest, out of conscious awareness.

As the world gets smaller and technology finds the seams of private lives, perhaps we are getting the deeper impressions of a comprehensive mindset, a structure that envelopes the athlete's competitive mindset, as well as his or her other roles. Further, maybe the time of separation of these roles and the willingness of psychology to segment experience into subject and object is coming to a crossroads. While it is the nature of the ego to compartmentalize, the arrow of development is aimed toward excellence and increasing complexity. This quality is the fullness and richness of development that is available to all of life's roles—not just when donning a uniform.

In working with athletes and families, I have developed a simple model for this end (see figures 1 and 2), so that the energy used in time and space is aligned with fundamental principles of character, achievement, and relationships. Instead of the athletic mindset being segmented, it is part of a comprehensive mindset that encompasses all experience and the motivation of our universal needs. After all, we always have the opportunity to develop our character, move towards goals, and deepen our relationships.

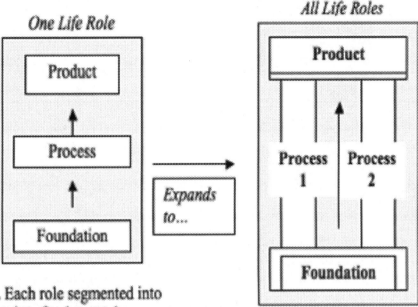

Figure 1. Each role segmented into three parts, i.e., fundamentals, process, and results for the role of the competitive athlete.

Figure 2. All roles flow from fundamental principles into processes. *Process 1* **(Individuation)** is the development of character and achievement; *Process 2* **(Integration)** is the development of relationships. Each pillar is fundamental to the structure of the outcome (product).

In Figure 1, we see a standard process of development of a life role. In the case of the athlete, the role of competitor is driven by the benchmarks of each level of competition. There are principles forming the foundation of the mindset, which give rise to the process or execution of these fundamentals. Finally, a result is achieved. This process feeds back on itself throughout the development of this life role. The athlete may adjust, work with a new coach, set new goals, etc. In this model, part of the athlete's mindset—or schema of how things work—includes the belief that who am I in the athletic endeavor is not who I am in life. There is a distinct boundary and, on the surface, one experience does not bleed into another. The public self and the private self can be subject to different internal beliefs (For example, cheating on the field is just part of the game, but it is not ok in life.)

Figure 2 offers a different perspective. The developmental path of becoming fully human involves two major processes that spiral upward and interweave. In *The Evolving Self*, Robert Kegan cites the processes of "Individuation" and "Integration" as directing development towards greater inclusiveness, complexity and coherence of personality. While the arrow of development is pointed this way, the path is not straight. There are times when we are developing more as an individual (achievement), but the tension will bring us back to integrate with a group and towards greater inclusiveness (relationships).

In this second model (Figure 2), all of life's roles are interconnected. The processes of development of character and healthy relationships weave within the process of achievement. So who you are on the field of competition is who you are in life. How you handle adversity in competition is how you handle the roadblocks of maturing or deepening your relationships. Do we meet these challenges with fairness, respect and grace, or look for something outside of us to blame?

While sport provides the competitive conditions to become more of an individual, the connection with others is always present. If you were to connect the athletic achievement with meaning, you would find mention of significant others. How many times have we seen champions receive their trophies and offer thanks to the many who have sacrificed and supported their journey? I will never forget the image of Pat Cash winning Wimbledon in 1987 and climbing the walls of Centre Court to be with his family and friends. Who could forget Phil Mickelson and his wife embracing after he won the 2010 Masters. Or Kim Clijsters holding her daughter as she celebrated her 2009 and 2010 US Open tennis championships. How many runners-up have sought the comfort of the inner circle after giving their all and coming up just short on that one outcome goal?

On a tacit level psychology has operated a level below this holistic view. Psychology has operated on the level of the mind, while placing a curtain over its origin as *the study of the soul*. The soul is more than thoughts and feelings, more than what we can operationalize and measure. The soul is the essence of the individual or as Merriam-Webster defines: *the total self or actuating cause of an individual life*.

Further, sports psychologists speak of self-efficacy and self-esteem as compartments that seemingly do not have penetrable barriers. "I do not have to value my life or feel good about myself in order to believe that I can sink this putt . . ." This perspective is understandable, for science seeks what is objective in order to measure. Yet, if you ask athletes about motivation and meaning, the subjective responses mirror Helen Keller's quote: "the best and most beautiful things in the world cannot be seen or touched . . . but are felt in the heart."

As we raise a new generation of competitors in a product-oriented society, perhaps we should take heed of a few of the high profile examples.

In recent times, professional golf has offered examples of compartmentalization in full view (John Daly and, recently, Tiger Woods) where the arrow of achievement seemed to be influenced by conflicts in the fundamentals of character and relationships. While it is not my place to judge, I do want to say that the reason we do not argue this conflict at length is because potential cannot truly be measured. We will never know what else Woods or Daly could have achieved . . . . (Note: Six months have past since this article appeared in its original form. Wood's struggles on and off the course in 2010 are now well documented.)

Potential exists at the fundamental level and the process is steeped in these foundational principles. We can measure results and use the tool of hindsight, but vision is about "proactive hindsight." We look to the future based on what intuitively deem is highest and best, and then work backward to the present to assess the gap. Integrity involves playing out decisions based on the principles that deliver the consequences. We use imagination and creativity to see if what we are doing and moving toward is honest and worthy. When we implement this process with conscience, it does not involve some arbitrary measure based in politics or personality. The latter often involves an attitude of entitlement and "not getting caught." The conscience is squelched, as the individual believes that the rules do not apply to him or her.

We are all recipients of this gift of vision, but often it is clouded by the trappings of ego. Pleasure, entertainment, adrenaline all feed the ego. What is worthwhile is not something short-lived or that will fade with time. These principle-based products of our current efforts then become the building blocks of an even greater future vision.

Any ego trapped in the manipulations of deceit and malice cannot be fully present. If you are giving less than yourself, there is a part of you that is affected by this incompleteness, for you are not aligned with the power of integrity. Science and psychology continue to expand, but currently do not have the answers when it comes to the matters of the heart. I suggest that our passion is weakened by lies and deceit hidden in the heart. Without this fuel, we are always less than . . . We do not have access to the full desire and pure process that turns potential into actual. The ego may have excuses such as, "I haven't found my swing." But, perhaps the answer to a lack of rhythm is something deeper, within the rhythm of human development.

Forgiveness is powerful; making amends is life long for trust can be lost in a moment. We can never measure potential lost.

Perhaps it is time to fully integrate the competitive mindset into a larger whole. Maybe it is time to stop making excuses and glamorizing those athletes who are written off as entertainers or take advantage of others. While drunken quarterbacks are great for newspapers and talk show ratings, there are many role models out there. As sports professionals and as parents, we can point this next generation towards athletes like Roger Federer, Mia Hamm, Derek Jeter and Drew Brees, all of whom exemplify the understanding of their place in causes larger than the individual. In other words, in their quest towards accomplishments, they have not diminished their character or their relationships.

Thinking of the competitive mindset as part of a comprehensive structure of character, relationships, *and* achievement will certainly be a healthier and more fulfilling developmental path for athletes—and leave fewer tragedies in its wake.

Keys to Mental Toughness

By John C. Panepinto, M.Ed, LPC, CSC

As competitive stakes rise and athletes push physical limits, there is a higher premium placed on the mental glue that enables athletes to hold it all together under pressure. This can be termed "mental toughness," and while athletes may have a certain innate level of this quality, it can be consistently improved as in the case of any other skill or attitude.

Mental toughness can be defined as a condition of the human mind that enables an athlete to adapt to challenges in all phases of competition in order to execute at peak performance levels. These challenges may be internal or external, such as the weather or the athlete's ability to bring his state of mind back to the present. A challenge may be improving a technique in practice or it may be the external distractions (media, new surroundings, etc.) leading up to an event. The challenge of competitive situations may involve playing from behind, with a lead or in a dead even heat. Regardless of the challenges or conditions, the athlete's present level of mental toughness will indicate how well he adapts to the challenge in the moment. Therefore, it becomes a key quality to develop and a key indicator of success.

Developing mental toughness is a two-pronged process in terms of coping and developing. This can be conceptualized as the development of competitive Intelligence (IQ) and competitive Resilience (EQ). Intelligence involves the athlete's systematic development of traits, skills, attitudes, and knowledge consistent with executing at peak performance levels in his sport.

Resilience (or competitive EQ) entails the development of the competitor's immune system with respect to adversity, as well as rising to meet the challenge of higher levels of execution and performance. The mentally tough athlete has the intelligence to learn to improve physically, emotionally, and mentally in order to achieve his vision. This means the athlete not only learns the intricacies of succeeding in his chosen sport, but also learns his own inner workings by continually becoming more self-aware. The mentally tough athlete also develops the resilience to adapt to challenges in all phases of competition (practice, pre-competition, etc.), and evolve with the challenge of pushing the present boundaries of his performance level.

As the athlete progresses on this dual path, he develops a mindset that serves this process of learning, experiencing, and reflecting. This system of beliefs, values, and expectations has been referred to as a "Champion's mindset," but the author prefers the term "High Performance Mindset." While championships and wins may be a results goal, a High Performance Mindset represents the process that will produce this result. It serves the expectation of being in control of one's own process regardless of the outcome.

A "High Performance" mindset is the body-mind intelligence that drives peak performance and:

- Is motivated by the process of consistently executing at its highest level.
- Is growth-oriented.
- Is driven by learning, experiencing and reflecting.
- Seeks consistent improvement.
- Allows the body's intelligence (unconscious competence) to react in the moment and understands why things work (conscious competence).
- Understands that adversity is part of competition and adapts to this.
- Focuses on what it can control.

The goal of the High Performance mindset is excellence, which is benchmarked at each level of each individual sport. This objective of excelling requires mental toughness and is a process that must receive the same intensity of focus and attention as the development of physical skills.

The diagram on the next page represents a visual of the developmental model of Mental Toughness:

Model of Mental Toughness

Intelligence (IQ)

* Vision
* Constant improvement
* Principles of excellence
* Know self

Resilience (EQ)

* Character
* Mind-set, skills, and attitude to handle challenges and adversity
* Belief in self

Balance/Change

Quality of Mental Toughness

In addition to my own competitive experience, twenty-five years of coaching and counseling led me to develop 11 Keys to help structure the process of becoming mentally tough. These Keys require an understanding of the principles and character traits that underlie the development of specific skills. Here are a few examples of "11 Keys to Mental Toughness":

❋ **Take Total Responsibility for Yourself**

An athlete's maturity level will dictate how to structure the development of these Keys, but this Key is foundational. It represents a vital inflection point in maturity and turns the athlete inward on the path to achievement. This principle is beyond setting and keeping goals and learning to focus attention. Responsibility dictates the ownership of experience and the development of an internal locus of control. It means becoming responsible for victories, defeats, and disassembling excuses and blame along the way. Regardless of outcome, the experience of practice and competition is used as a content to continuously improve.

❋ **Positive Self-talk**

Self-talk influences your internal environment. It is your inner voice that helps you problem-solve, assess risk, regulate emotions, and make decisions. Self-talk can also stimulate positive mental states that serve execution. You get to choose how the coach in your head sounds. Mentally tough athletes choose a positive and productive voice. This key is beyond affirmations and positive thinking for the athlete is not absorbed in the "feeling" of the internal dialogue. Rather the athlete is mindful of her inner voice and regulating self in the present.

❋ **Be In "Player Mode"**

In my experience as an athlete and as a coach, I have come to identify three distinct states that are related to the quality of performance. These states or "modes" are driven by three different processes and require athletes to develop the skill of self-awareness and an elementary knowledge of how their brains work.

In the first of these three modes, "Survivor Mode," the athlete's execution is being driven by fear. All fear is based in survival and loss. We are wired as human to respond to this fear by fighting, "flighting", or freezing. Each of these actions is comparably short term because they are fueled by adrenaline. Most competitions of any duration cannot be fueled by adrenalin because this hormone simply wears you out. An adrenalin rush is just that and is followed by a crash. What is more important, we are as far from the part of our brain that regulates, creates, solves problems, intuits, sequences, analyses language and space, and processes globally, as we could possibly be. Optimal performance requires these mental functions to execute at a high level. A test to help you discover if you are in the Survivor Mode is:

- You feel tight, and feel a lack of rhythm.
- Your breathing may be short and labored.
- You have tunnel vision, and may find it difficult to remember the details (What's the score?").
- You experience soreness more than usual following the competition.

In "Emotional Mode" the competitor is riding the peaks and valleys of emotionalized energy. In this mode it is too difficult to be consistent, relaxed, and steady in thought and emotion. While you need emotions, you cannot be absorbed by them. It is fine to have reactions and fine to enjoy your efforts, but when your effort revolves around emotions, you will perform in a less than optimum state because you are not in the present. When you emote, your thought processes are often tied to a past or future event. So if you are angry, you are angry at something that happened rather than what is happening. Anger has to be stoked and it is stoked with thoughts of what evoked the anger. When you are anxious you are thinking of what might happen (future) and what you have no control over. When you are excessively excited, again you are excited about what you have done or may do rather than what is occurring in the present. To celebrate you recall the accomplishment (or fantasize about the finish line), yet the competition continues in the present and requires your attention in the present. A test to help you discover if you are in the Emotional Mode is:

- You sense a change in your energy level.
- You keep recycling thoughts.
- Your emotions are telling you what to do rather than you being in control of your emotions.
- You often regret what has happened when you come to be in the present.

In "Player Mode" we have all the faculties of high performance in our consciousness. We are energizing the part of our brain that regulates, creates, problem-solves, adapts, analyses, processes globally, intuits, and allows muscle memory to unfold unconsciously. We are contently absorbed in the process of executing. We flow between effort and demand and notice how well we execute without being absorbed in the energy of emotions. We have emotions, but are not defined by the emotion or immersed in it. Rather, the emotion motivates the action and the state of mind. We are present, performing in the here and now. Our mind is calm and acutely alert (focused), we are intelligently performing, our bodies are relaxed (tension-free) and aroused (energized to the appropriate level), and we are resilient to what does not go our way without getting sidetracked by our reactions to setbacks.

❀ Reflect On Your Goals

Goals without active reflection on their meaning and adjustment for progress often do not work. Unless you *make* time for reflection, schedule demands and technological distractions can limit your opportunities. Without this Key, "burnout" can occur because it is in the process of reflection that we come to know that for which we are grateful. Without gratitude, entitlement rears its head.

❀ Believe In Yourself

Belief in self is linked to the athlete's path and purpose, and provides the fuel of passion. Without passion, you will not do the little things in tired moments. Belief in the self provides immunity to doubt, self-sabotage, and the need for approval. Belief in self also motivates the athlete to work from strengths, rather than being driven by fear or trying to be perfect.

❋ Know What to Do With Your Emotions

Failure is often due to a faulty plan or ineffectively dealing with adversity. The first is a mistake of intelligence, the second a lack of resilience.

Athletes react to situations regardless of how present they are. This emotional reflex does not require thought; therefore a thoughtful *response* to the situation matters most. If your reaction *is* always your response, then this implies inflexibility. Mentally tough competitors learn that some reactions come from an unconscious level. There are some reactions you "expect" and some you are unaware of because they exist on a level you may not have access to until you meet the moment.

If you are not conscious of your reactions, you will not be in control of your choices. Control your emotional process or your emotions will control you.

❋ No Surrender

Develop a philosophy of "always finish what you start—with your best." Quitting requires you to give up what you have control of: attitude, effort and focus. When you choose to quit you suffer the loss on a different level, because quitting is not a momentary process. The effect ripples into the future because you must let go of motivation and meaning before you can rationalize the option of quitting.

These are a few of the *Keys to Mental Toughness*. Know that athletes are always in process and can improve in their ability to meet the challenges of competition. Developing a structure and philosophy of meeting the moment with intelligence and resilience will help athletes to be at their best and execute to their highest level when it matters most.

About the Author:

John Panepinto is a Licensed Professional Counselor, a National Certified Counselor, and a Certified Sports Counselor recognized by the International Sports Professionals Association. He is a consultant for developmental issues to parents and teachers in the largest school system in North Carolina.

John is a Certified Teaching Professional (Professional Tennis Registry) and has coached top-ranked juniors, college players, and satellite professionals. In nearly three decades of coaching and counseling, he has worked with several champions and elite athletes. He has worked with athletes in many sports on developing a high performance mindset and mental toughness. John has also authored several works on Mental Toughness, available at DxSportsPerformance.com.

John competed in several sports including Open Level Racquetball. John won over 50 titles, as well as regional and state championships, and competed in professional events.

SPORTS
HEALTH

Concussions: Invisible Injuries

By Robert Andrews, MA, LMFT, CSC

There has been much attention given to the topic of sports concussions over the last few weeks. Mike Leach the head football coach at Texas Tech University was suspended and later fired over his alleged treatment of Adam James, a Tech player who suffered a mild concussion. Adam happens to be the son of ESPN analyst Craig James. Recently the NFL and Congress have created committees to discuss the treatment of concussions, and the link between head injuries in sports and long-term brain damage.

Not Your Normal Sports Injury

I for one am glad to hear this. Concussions are a different type of injury and are not as easily detected as other injuries. Unlike a knee injury, a broken arm, or a separated shoulder, there is no apparent physical evidence that anything is wrong with the athlete when they suffer a concussion. With knee injuries or other obvious sports related injuries there are crutches, knee braces, slings, or cast that tell doctors, coaches, teammates, trainers, and fans that something serious has happened to the athlete. It is obvious that rehabilitation and time are required for healing to take place and for the athlete to be able to return to competition.

What is a Concussion?

Concussions are in effect a bruising of the brain. When an athlete suffers helmet-to-helmet contact, or hits their head on the field or court the brain slams against the skull (which can cause bruising). The more serious the concussion, the more serious the resulting swelling and bruising of the brain tissue can be. This swelling and bruising causes memory loss, headaches, poor reaction time, impaired thinking, confusion, slow recall, and other serious symptoms.

Current Treatment

Treatment requires literally turning the brain off. Athletes are required to stay out of school, stay away from television, computers, video games, or other activities that create stress on the damaged brain. IMPACT testing is utilized to identify deficiencies in brain functioning. This test also shows when the athletes brain functioning returns to normal levels. Physical activity is monitored looking for symptoms like headaches, dizziness, and nausea. When the athlete is symptom free and testing shows a return to normal levels of brain functioning the treating physician and athletic trainer give the green light to return to competition.

The Psychology of Sports Injuries

I believe that there is a psychological component to concussions as well. In my work with injured athletes I have found that athletes who suffer concussions all experience intense mental and emotional reactions to their experiences. In most cases these reactions are traumatic.

I have worked with athletes who have been hit so hard they were out cold for over a minute. Some have no memory of the hit that knocked them out, but they have images in their mind that are created from what people tell them happened, or what they see on game film. They talk about the terrible confusion, fear, and embarrassment they feel when they recall sitting on the bench knowing something very serious has happened but not remembering anything about the injury. These images are incredibly vivid and disturbing to the athlete.

Other athletes have very clear memories of the experience. They have told me what it was like to be strapped to a stretcher, immobilized, and taken by ambulance to the hospital. I have heard numerous stories from athletes who return to play, threw numerous interceptions, and were booed off the field. These experiences are all filled with incredible intensity and have a profound impact on the mental and emotional state of the athlete. These same athletes also tell me about coaches, teammates, and fans that tease, ridicule and humiliate them for sitting out of practice and games.

Sports injuries, particularly concussions are never just physical in nature. When we create a space for the injured athlete to tell their story and help them process and integrate the psychological impact and trauma of the concussion, athletes get better. Their "lights turn back on". Their mind clears and their self-confidence returns.

Now imagine Adam James standing in a dark shed for three hours, unable to sit down or lean against anything. What was the message being sent to him and other Tech athletes who might suffer a concussion? I can't imagine anything therapeutic coming from this type of treatment. Imagine the pressure put on the athletic trainers to follow orders demanding this type of treatment for an athlete. Sadly, this story sounds like so many other stories I have heard about the treatment of a concussed athlete. This treatment was meant to humiliate, degrade, and punish Adam for sitting out of practice with a concussion.

Time For Change

It took Adam being the son of a high profile, nationally recognized sports analyst to bring attention to the treatment his son endured after suffering a concussion.

Along with the NFL playoffs, bowl games, and the BCS National Championship, the eyes and ears of the sports world are now focused on the treatment of athletes who suffer concussions. I am elated to hear that mandatory guidelines are being put in place by the NFL for teams to follow when providing care for athletes who suffer a concussion. I hope the NCAA and high schools throughout the country follow their lead.

These injuries are real and very serious. The athlete who suffers a concussion deserves to be treated with the same care and dignity as any athlete who suffers any other type of sports related injury.

Sports Injuries:
Throwing A Stone In A Pond

By Robert Andrews, MA, LMFT, CSC

My work in the world of sports psychology is very rewarding and exciting. I am blessed to work with some of the best athletes in the country. I am fortunate to see them achieve tremendous highs in their careers as athletes. Unfortunately I see many of them after they have experienced devastating lows. These lows come from poor performances, or in some cases a serious sports related injury. Some of the time I see an athlete after they have suffered an injury, but often I am present when an athlete is injured. Through my trained eye I can see the impact of the injury on the athlete, and the athlete's system.

A sport related injury happens to the athlete, but impacts many others in this system. By system I mean the support team of the athlete. Parents, grandparents, siblings, teammates, coaches, trainers, instructors, teachers, and friends are all profoundly affected by the injury.

I was at a baseball game a few weeks ago and a player was hit in the head with a fastball. He went down hard. When the pitch hit him there was a collective moan from the crowd. In an instant his coaches and trainers were around him. When they got to him he was in pretty bad shape. Most of the crowd was on their feet watching. Many had their hands on their heads hoping he was all right. His teammates gathered outside the dugout, held hands and prayed. The opposing team gathered around the pitchers mound and consoled the pitcher.

He was very upset. The batter lay motionless on home plate for about 5 minutes. When his legs began to move people began to chatter quietly. He was carted off the field on a stretcher and taken by ambulance to the emergency room. There was a loud ovation from the crowd and after the ambulance drove off play was resumed. The pitcher took a new ball from the catcher, everyone sat down again, and play resumed. Or so we think.

When something like this happens it is like taking a huge stone and throwing it into a calm pond. When the stone hits he water it makes a big splash. The waves from this splash work their way around the pond until they reach the shore. The waves continue to rock the pond until the shore absorbs their energy.

With a serious sports related injury the waves affect everyone in the athlete's life. Imagine what it must be like for the parent of the player who was hit to see their son face down in the dirt after being hit in the head with a 90 mph fastball. First there is the waiting, the silence, more waiting and then a transport to the hospital. Teammates, coaches, friends, girlfriends, trainers, even the opposing pitcher are all suffer the same intense reaction to the injury.

For many the waves in the pond never calm down. They keep on rocking the once still waters, the inner world of the athlete, and those in the athletes system. In one minute the athlete is strong, powerful, prepared, and the next they are on the ground wondering if they are going to live, much less play baseball again. These waves reverberate within the family members, friends, and teammates too.

I feel fortunate when I am able to treat an athlete who has suffered this type of injury. They recover and put the injury behind them. They regain confidence, return to a high level of play, and in the process of recovery become wiser, and more mature.

Parents and others in the system are profoundly affected by these types of injuries. When they sit in the stands for the first time and watch their son or daughter get back in the batters box they are a nervous wreck. Parents have reported experiencing sweaty palms, elevated heart rates, and high levels of anxiety.

I worked with a quarterback who suffered a serious concussion. I was talking with his father minutes before his son's first game back. His father said that he had talked with the coach and that they were going to start him off very slowly with a simple playbook for that game. I asked him why? He said he was still coming along and needed to come back slowly. I looked him right in the eye and said, "Your son is fine now and will play a great game. Whatever is going on with you about his injury is yours to deal with now." After a pause he said, "your right, I am terrified he is going to get hurt again."

This is a very normal response for the parent of an injured athlete. After an injury parents usually treat their injured athlete differently. They might be excessively concerned, watchful, and protective. Once an athlete has returned to play and parents continue to treat them this way it can have a very negative affect the athlete. It serves as a constant reminder that they have been injured. Nothing is spoken, but the athlete senses the tension, fear, and anxiety that is humming inside of their parents. They unconsciously feel this when they are competing.

When parents come in to see me after their son or daughter is injured it is a very powerful experience for them. To download the horrific images they carry, and rid themselves of the fear, anxiety, and trauma that lingers is transformational for them. They are able to sit in the stands and enjoy the game and watch their athlete play at a high level again. The waves in the pond have calmed down and they are at peace.

Next time you are at a sporting event and see an injury take place look at the situation through this lens of perception. The impact on the system is profound.

About the Author:

Robert Andrews, M.A., founder and director of The Institute of Sports Psychology®, has been in private practice as a sports psychology consultant and psychotherapist for 18 years. His areas of expertise, primary areas of focus and passion are working with athletes to help them realize their peak potential as an athlete, helping injured athletes overcome the emotional, mental, and spiritual effects of their sports related injury and teaching coaches how to coach at their best when things are at their worst.

Robert played on a Texas State Championship football team and as an athlete suffered his own serious sports related injuries in high school and college. As a psychotherapist, he received extensive training in performance enhancement, and trauma resolution. He began to realize the extensive impact of sports injuries on performance and how these injuries hold athletes back not only in sports, but also in life. The Institute of Sports Psychology is the culmination of his dream to dramatically impact the way performance and recovery is addressed and treated in athletes.

Whey Protein may be Risky;
Liquid Protein may be Optimal

By Elaine Hastings, RD, LD/N, CSSD
Edited by W. Rusty Dunham, BSPharm., PharmD.

It's always best to meet daily nutritional requirements by simply eating good, healthy food. However, there are circumstances, when this is difficult, inconvenient or nearly impossible. Consider the long-distance runner, who "hits the wall" at 20 miles, or the middle-aged woman, who needs to maintain lean muscle but can't afford extra calories.

Many people assume that a protein supplement is only beneficial to serious athletes or bodybuilders, but that couldn't be farther from the truth. Protein has many uses, and supplementation can be beneficial for a wide variety of users, including; the elderly; those with joint or degenerative diseases, or orthopedic conditions; the overweight; people who do heavy manual labor in their work, sport or hobby; those going through growth phases; people in physical rehabilitation; adults who work out on a regular basis; teen athletes who are trying to build muscle and strength; people pain or inflammation issues; or anyone with pain resulting from excessive joint stress.

The trick is getting extra protein without absorbing those extra calories, and subjecting the body to bulky or bloating fillers. One popular source of protein supplementation is whey protein powder, a liquid by-product of cheese production, commonly added to shakes by athletes and others trying to gain muscle. Whey may also be added to our "nondairy" food products during production and preparation. Nondairy products may also contain lactose. If you know—or even suspect—that you or someone you're coaching or treating is lactose intolerant, then spend some time reading product labels. Any of the following ingredients mean the product has lactose: dry milk solids, nonfat dry milk powder, milk by-products, curds, and whey. It's also good to know that dairy products which are "fat reduced" or "fat free" generally present higher lactose, as do low fat foods, which often incorporate dairy solids. This is part of what makes trying a dairy-free lifestyle so difficult. If a person is lactose sensitive or lactose intolerant, ingesting whey protein can cause great discomfort including abdominal discomfort, belly cramps, diarrhea, nausea, itchiness or watery eyes, and possibly asthma attacks.

Lactose intolerance is different from a milk allergy, but people often confuse the two because the symptoms can be identical. Lactose intolerant people do not produce enough of the enzyme lactase, which is needed to break down the sugar in milk. It is estimated that 75% of all people decrease in production of lactase during adulthood. This intolerance may increase during childhood, particularly for Mexican Americans who jump from 18% intolerant at age two to a whopping 47% by age 10, leading to many potential intestinal problems. The more you consume, the more severe the symptoms would be.

To help sort through the nutrition labels, get familiar with the most common dairy ingredients present in foods. Whey is present in a variety of processed and prepared food products. Whey protein is composed of lactalbumin and lactalglobulin, and is found in both food products and health supplements. Other common forms of whey present in food products are sweet whey, whey powder, whey protein, whey protein concentrate, and whey protein hydrolysate.

An alternative protein supplementation for lactose intolerant, athletes, exercisers, body builders and people who want to gain lean muscle is using collagen instead of whey as the source of protein. It can be taken before, during and after activity: to pre-load before a workout, during extended activity for endurance and decreased fatigue or to help with recovery after exercise. It's important that the liquid collagen is from a high-quality source, tested and is a complete protein with added tryptophan.

Check the label and be sure the collagen protein you are choosing contains NO added whey. Some "newer" collagen proteins, such as AminoRip®, contain NO lactose, NO dairy, NO carbs, NO fats, NO sugar, NO high fructose corn syrup (HFCS), NO sorbitol, NO gluten, NO soy, and NO whey.

Another reason to pay attention to your choice of protein supplement is contamination. In 2010, Consumer Reports tests found that some "protein shakes" exceeded United States Pharmacopeia (USP) standards for exposure to heavy metals when three or more servings were consumed a day due to contamination during processing. Failing the heavy metal test were some of our most popular protein shakes, including EAS's Myoplex and Cytosport's Muscle Milk.

I was exposed to alternative proteins early on. Before I was a registered dietitian, I was a competitive gymnast. I married a bodybuilder who worked as a high school coach; his "kids" were always looking to build muscle and strength. I've personally worked with a wide variety of professional and competitive athletes, and my hospital patients often have a need for protein. The common thread that runs through all these stories is the protein. I've spent years comparing the various forms in which it's available.

It was my work as a registered dietitian, however, that gave me one of those "aha" moments. It had to do with collagen, a form of protein. Over a ten-year period, I had prescribed a liquid collagen protein that was available through the hospitals that employed me. My patients, who had incurred burns and wounds, healed much faster when given a regimen including this form of protein. The specific product used where I worked was made from pork collagen, which most closely resembles the human skeletal muscles. The phenomenal successes I witnessed made me an advocate for the product. But because of my background and my lifestyle, I began to see other applications for this form of protein.

I thought that if collagen could help a wound heal; it could also help a muscle heal from being broken down in a workout. Collagen protein aids the repair of muscle tissue. Since a good workout or physical exercise is actually breaking down the body's muscles, I believe collagen protein assists in the rebuilding process. Collagen makes it possible to heal faster, while building leaner muscle, following a workout. Some people even find they sleep more soundly when taking collagen protein. Sounds better all the time, doesn't it?

My husband and I discussed collagen many times—the registered dietitian and the bodybuilder/coach, brainstorming away—as to how the collagen my hospital made available was different from other protein powders, bars or liquid proteins on the market. Its bioavailability was a big part of what made it unique, and this is a big factor in protein ingestion.

A powder form can provide extra protein without as much work for the body, but comes with the added calories and unnecessary fillers of what it's poured into. A liquid protein supplement may be a better choice. Find one that's low in calories, and hydrolyzed—or "predigested"—which simply means that you ingest it in its smallest form, with no extra work for the body to break it down.

I realized the hydrolyzed collagen I was prescribing for my patients was a pure, powerful protein: ready to heal, ready to build lean muscle, ready to rejuvenate skin, bodies, and lifestyles. So we decided to bring the same product to the consumer market, tweaking it so the famously nasty taste of liquid protein was no longer an issue.

I've seen this particular collagen product endorsed by a former Mr. America, a former MLB player, trail runners, triathletes, countless high school coaches and teen athletes, 55 year old men who have lost their bellies and 50 year old women who have found their "back fat" disappearing without changing their workouts have attributed their success to liquid collagen protein. Even a 61 year old whose hip replacement didn't heal correctly reports no pain if drinking 3 ounces daily.

Although most people I know are not taking liquid collagen internally specifically for their skin, department stores and websites are making a great deal of money selling collagen for external use. From personal and anecdotal experience I have discovered that when ingested, liquid collagen changes the skin quickly and dramatically, producing a healthier looking softer skin with fewer razor burns.

As we age, our body slowly stops producing collagen protein, and it's collagen that gives our skin elasticity. While collagen is effective in treating skin trauma, such as burns and wounds, and in helping muscles to heal and rebuild, it also greatly affects the hair, nails and overall healthy appearance of skin, leading to its use in high-end skin care products. The appearance of dry, wrinkled skin is really the lack of collagen.

Supplementing your athlete's, patient's or team's diet, with a natural source of collagen protein doesn't just make them more youthful looking, however. Collagen can help build lean healthy muscle—the muscle of youth—as well as healthy joints and bones. For many years, there has been a debate on over how much protein athletes, exercises and body builders require. RDAs are set to avoid malnutrition and are considered the minimum needed, NOT what the body needs for maximum or optimal performance. A body that does not get enough protein will actually start to cannibalize its own muscles as a source of protein. A higher protein intake can preserve lean muscle.

To date, I haven't found another product which can aid in building lean muscle, speed recovery and give endurance, without extra calories, sugar, bloat, or lactose issues. And my credentials are on the line when I share with you that my son's pediatrician asked—when charting an impressive muscle gain—if he was being given human growth hormone. At that point, my husband and I knew we had to have our particular product tested and certified to be free from all banned substances, which it has been, by Informed Choice. All parents and coaches should be very aware of what supplements their teens are taking, as stimulants and steroids are a big issue across the entire country today.

I encourage you to investigate low-calorie collagen protein supplements. See what's out there; see what kind of results you can get for people you know. My hospitalized patients have benefited for years, and now I'm seeing the benefit for active adults and athletes, all because of liquid collagen protein.

About the Author:

Sports nutrition authority Elaine Hastings, RD, LD/N, CSSD is owner of Associates in Nutrition in southwest Florida. She is a popular go-to media source on the subject of nutrition and also the Chief Scientific Officer for AminoRip® International Corp. Mrs. Hastings is currently developing an online wellness portal, and her newspaper column is incorporated into her blog on sports nutrition. She is presently working on a book about sports nutrition.

SPORTS
COMMENTARY & MEDIA

Pro Athletes & Sports Broadcasting

By Kurt A. David

"100% of Professional Athletes Ultimately Experience Job Termination," I frequently chant. 25% are bankrupt within the first year out, 60% to 80% get divorced, and over 75% go broke within two years out.

As Creator, Host, and Executive Producer of the ***FROM GLORY DAYS TV SHOW*** I've the honor of sitting down with many former professional athletes. I've listened to the personal stories of Hall of Fame, All-star, and World Champion former athletes as they've transitioned from the pinnacle of their pro sports careers back into normal, everyday lives. Needless to say, I'm unable to take my hosting position lightly, but because of much preparation and focus I'm able to enjoy the process throughout.

If there's one thing I've learned from my friends . . . . preparation is the foundation of any sports broadcast. Detroit Pistons TV broadcasters, Greg Kelser and George Blaha have taught me this the most. The hours of prep they put into every NBA broadcast inspired me to be as thorough with my own TV show. Simply showing up at the studio to interview my guests just doesn't happen. Once our guests are secured I'll spend hours per athlete, scouring their sports history from high school through their final days as a professional, looking for any fact or angle that would make interesting conversation.

As an example, I was able to find a minor detail about 1984 World Series Champion Detroit Tiger, Dave Bergman and posed it as an opening question for the show. The question was just enough to cause Dave to pause and think, and then opened a floodgate of dialogue about this detail and beyond. In that moment my hours of research paid off.

Another example came during my research for Episode 4 when I discovered NCAA Champion and former NBA star, Terry Mills had a post sports involvement in drag racing. Imagining a 6'10" body strapped inside a low flying rocket and racing down a quarter-mile track made for some great discussion while being insightful and entertaining to our studio audience and viewers.

Not all of my preparation finds humor or fun facts about my guests, as discovered when interviewing a former NFL quarterback in Episode 6. Sadly, this guest's transition from sports included bankruptcy, jail, and the suicide of his 15-year-old son. Our discussion took great sensitivity on my part while the tape was rolling, but ultimately led to my guest sharing his current involvement as an advocate for depression as he travels and speaks throughout the country.

I also discovered no matter how much time I spend on preparation, sometimes things just happen and I have to go with the flow. This couldn't have been truer than during Episode 2 and my interview with 1968 World Series Champion, Jim Northrup. Partway through our taping we got onto the topic of dairy farming (Jim grew up on a farm, but also worked in the cattle business following his pro sports career). In response to his comment, 'anyone can milk a cow'

I simply responded with doubt of my own ability. To the studio audience and my surprise, Jim elaborated about the process including details of grabbing the 'tits' of the cow and pulling until milk starting coming out. Once I stopped laughing out loud I regrouped and continued the interview, trusting our fine editing crew would eloquently remove his explicative of the cow's certain anatomy. When I see this particular clip now I can't help but laugh again, but understand preparation is not simply enough and a second key item is needed.

The second key element, along with preparation, is the ability to focus, tuning-in to the moment while listening to every word and phrase. Remaining disciplined and controlling my thoughts from wondering more than one or two questions ahead. This conscious choice allows me to live in the moment, waiting to pounce on an elaborative opportunity that might normally be glossed over or missed. I find this skill particularly important since many professional athletes have vast media experience and tend to go into "media mode" or autopilot.

My ability to focus and remain in the moment gave me the opportunity to inquire further on Episode 1 with NCAA Champion and former NBA player, Greg Kelser. As mentioned earlier, Greg is now an NBA TV broadcaster and no-doubt a media pro. Not only did I have the challenge of trying to get Greg out of "media mode" from his days as a professional athlete, but even more so as someone who is in front TV cameras on a daily basis. I opened the show by asking what it's like being on the other side of the microphone, being interviewed, versus interviewing others like he now does professionally. Greg was quick to respond, "I'm very comfortable over here because I simply need to answer the questions, I don't have to think them up." Focusing on the word, 'comfortable' I sprung immediately into another angle of the same question, asking what the most uncomfortable he's been as a broadcaster on my side of the microphone. From this question we were able to listen as Greg shared his challenges as a broadcaster that I'm convinced we wouldn't have heard if I glossed past this opportunity and went on with my next line of questioning.

Listening demonstrates our ability to focus and during Episode 8 it wasn't me but a studio audience member who listened intently to our NFL Super Bowl Champion guest. As a result, the audience member was able to ask an insightful question during our studio audience "Q & A" segment of the show, which lead into a revealing answer about the Super Bowl game that I didn't even know.

Being the host of the *FROM GLORY DAYS TV SHOW* is a very rewarding and enjoyable position. I'm unable to imagine doing anything else in the TV business right now, but understand the amount of preparation and focus it takes for each broadcast to be successful. Lessons I've learned from others who've been there before, and lessons that allow me to enjoy the process that much more.

"100% of Professional Athletes Ultimately Experience Job Termination"

By Kurt A. David

We must face it, there's no denying it, but the question is . . . are we prepared to handle it? I'm talking about *CHANGE*, of course, and, as the saying goes, it's the inevitable constant in life.

People *change*, circumstances *change*, seasons *change*, and the list of *changes* are unending. As an example, "*100% of Professional Athletes Ultimately Experience Job Termination,*" I've always said. This is an undeniable fact. During the process of this transition twenty-five percent become bankrupt within the first year out of pro sports; over seventy-five percent of NFL players go broke within the first two years out and up to eighty percent experience divorce. Needless to say, this *change* for professional athletes can be difficult. But, facing great adversity during *change* is not limited to high caliber athletes.

The 18th Amendment forced over one thousand businesses to drastically *change*. Over 1,200 breweries existing in America at the beginning of Prohibition could no longer legally sell their goods. Most were unable to face this imposed *change* and closed their doors during the course of this law's enactment. Only 244 remained as a direct result. Needless to say, this *change* for breweries had its devastating effects.

I'd be remised to only dwell on undesirable *change* since it can be good, the spice of life. There are times in our lives when *change* is not only welcomed but embraced and considered a fresh breath of life. *Change* can even bring us a new lease on life, and has done exactly that for many who've made adjustments in their lifestyle and daily practice.

Regardless of whether *change* is good, bad, wanted, or undesired, change happens. This is an inexorable fact. Perhaps focusing on the reasons or desirability of *change* is, therefore, not as important as how we handle it. History is peppered with attempts at handling *change,* some having been successful, and some leaving a great deal more to be desired.

So, what makes for successful transition? What allows people to embrace victory while facing *change* and adversity in their personal and professional lives? Through my research and experience I've discovered five things people have done throughout sports and history to successfully face to adapt in their personal and professional lives.

1. REFOCUS

Refocusing is the first element in effectively facing *change*. The best way to refocus is to evaluate your current goals and then set new ones. As an example, five-time NHL All-star John Ogrodnick began refocusing his life long before his transition from professional sports began. Understanding that his years as a high caliber athlete were numbered, Ogrodnick evaluated his current status and started to prepare for the next phase of his life, the one that followed pro sports, by setting new goals in areas of financial advising. By the time Ogrodnick finished his NHL career, he was equipped for the paramount *change* of exiting sports by establishing these new goals in preparation for what lay ahead of him. In addition, these new goals assisted in establishing a new sense of purpose, something imperative when redeveloping passion in people's lives.

2. USE NETWORK

Once a refocusing has occurred I've discovered successful transitioning means tapping into the network of people we've all created in order to seek assistance toward our goals. I cannot personally think of a better example than NBA Hall of Famer, Dave Bing. High school and collegiate All-American, #1 Draft pick, eight-time NBA All-star, and revered as one of the "50 best NBA players of all time," Bing created a vast network of people throughout his athletic career. This he is carried over into the next phase of his life as businessperson and now Mayor of a major metropolitan city. To this day he continues to draw from this vast list of people in order to accomplish his ever-progressing goals.

3. LET GO

Arguably, letting go may be the most difficult aspect of *change*. We are creatures of comfort and habit. Not *changing* our behavioral tendencies can be the foundation for difficulties when facing inevitable *change*. Case in point: for thirteen years Anheuser-Busch understood they could no longer legally sell beer under the Prohibition Act. They were confronted with either not *changing* and the ultimate closing of their doors, or letting go of the fact that they had been a brewery and were now faced with finding a way to *change* and, thus, survive (history has clearly conveyed the direction they took ultimately establishing them as the number one brewery in the world with over $16 billion in annual sales). Additional case in point are the athletes who hang on way beyond the pinnacles of their careers and do not *change*, eventually departing their craft on a less than stellar note. Athletes who should have retired years before they did or, when having done so, seek to return to the spotlight when remaining retired was really the best course to follow. Charles Barkley, Michael Jordan, Evander Holyfield, Rickey Henderson, and Gaylord Perry are just a handful of professional athletes who, arguably, fall under this category. No matter the names, the point is clear. Move on!

4. EXECUTE

"Knowing what to do isn't good enough, if you don't have the discipline to do it," a wise coach once told me. And, of course, we all know the best kind of discipline is self-discipline. Possessing that during the process of *change* can sometimes be the difference between facing *change* and embracing it. Knowing the keys to success are only as good as their application.

5. SOMEONE

Have you heard it said that man is not an island? Nor should he be when looking *change* dead in the eye. Misery finds company, but it also finds comfort. Finding someone to share, encourage, and lead you through *change* can be a very powerful thing. One particular NBA TV Broadcaster still speaks gratefully about the people who assisted his *change* from pro athlete to normal, everyday life following his sports career. Greg Kelser often spent time in the studio learning from experienced TV broadcasters. After his days as a professional basketball player Kelser attached himself to these mentors and, by doing so, kept busy. This not only allowed him the time to gradually face this major *change* in his life, but also accelerate his TV broadcasting career in the process.

Whether we like it or not, *change* is in the air. The question is not if whether we will ever face *change* but how. Are we equipped to handle it? Hopefully, you are better prepared now for when it is your turn at bat.

About the Author:

Kurt A. David played professional basketball in Europe and now possesses an advanced degree in counseling. His bestselling book, *FROM GLORY DAYS—Successful Transitions of Professional Detroit Athletes*, chronicles the lives of some Hall of Fame, All-star, and World Champion former Detroit Pistons, Tigers, Red Wings, and Lions as they've transitioned from pro sports careers back into normal, everyday lives. Kurt possesses solid experience with TV, Radio, and Print media, which includes appearances on Sirius XM Radio, CBS, ABC, and NBC affiliates, as well as articles in Men's Health Magazine, and much more. Kurt A. David resides in Metro Detroit with his wife and two young daughters where he's a Diplomat Credentialed *Internationally Certified Sports Counselor* by the ISPA*, Bestselling Author, Transition Consultant for Professional & Olympic Athletes, and TV Host/Executive Producer of the FROM GLORY DAYS SHOW.* You can find out more at: www.fromglorydays.com

Manute Bol: A "Special Blessing"

By Joel Freeman

Manute Bol (7'7" NBA player) gave to those who had absolutely no way of repaying him for his time, energy and generosity. Fighting for a group of people tortured, slaughtered and misled by the government of Sudan. What a legacy of kindness, perseverance and courage Manute has left to the world!

On June 19, 2010 Manute Bol (47) died from a host of health conditions in a Virginia hospital. It was the combination of kidney failure, Stevens-Johnson Syndrome and internal bleeding that finally caused his heart to stop beating—all related to deferring much-needed health care in order to stay in Sudan to help through the April elections.

The number of articles, news stories and blogs reveals the outpouring of love and international attention focused on this gentle giant's legacy—not only as an NBA player, but also on the all-consuming drive he had to help his people back home in Sudan.

Allow me to take a step back: I was mentor/chaplain for the NBA Washington Bullets/Wizards for 19 years (1979-1998). How I became chaplain during the heyday of Kevin Porter, Elvin Hayes, Kevin Grevey, Bernard King, Wes Unseld, Jeff Ruland, Rick Mahorn, John Lucas, Chris Webber, Mitch Kupchak, and Manute Bol is another story.

The Washington Bullets drafted Manute in the second round in 1985. Nothing I had heard or read about him could have prepared me for what I saw—a tall, spindly man as thin as a praying mantis. My first thought was: *How is he going to survive the required running up and down the court, coupled with sharp elbows and all of the pounding that goes on under the basket?* I knew that no NBA opponent was going to give him a break. The team management putManute on a strict regimen weight lifting, pizza and anything else that would put some meat on his bones. He added 17 pounds before his debut in October 1985.

Manute's likeability factor and ticket-selling, shot-blocking statistics (2,086 blocks in 624 games over 10 seasons) speak for themselves. His physical presence, coupled with his famous trash-talking, warrior-like ferocity on the court forced other players to change their game. Somehow he defied all of the odds against him. Chuck Douglas (Assistant GM, Player Personnel Director, and Director of Scouting; 20 years for Bullets/Wizards) was fresh out of college and was assigned to deal with all media intrigued with Manute and also to take care of anything Manute needed to have done. He was on call 24/7. Chuck's first year, the Bullets invented a title for him: Public Relations and Coaching Assistant. It was cross-cultural miscommunication at its finest. Throw in a couple of video cameras and it would have been the gold standard for all other reality TV shows! Imagine the comedy. Manute had no license. No car. No apartment. No furniture. Nothing taught in any of the fine classes at the University of Maryland could prepare Chuck for this experience. Chuck was so young that he didn't have a clue about balancing a check book, what kind of curtains were needed to go with the furniture, and all sorts of other taken-for-granted mundane aspects of life in America. A cross-cultural accident waiting to happen on a daily basis.

Manute didn't have many clothes that fit him, so that first year he wore his Bullets practice gear most of the time. His contract called for the Bullets to pay him $137,500 that first season, so they helped out with much of the extra expenses. When Manute came to the NBA he could barely speak English and was having a tough time trying to explain his needs and also trying to comprehend the responses. One day Manute told Chuck that he had some small animals in his apartment that were eating his food and that he wanted to kill them. After trying to clarify the request, Chuck told him that he would take care of it. Chuck thought that the animals were mice or some other rodent, so he went out to pick up a few mouse traps, some other items and even a BB gun . . . just in case. When Manute saw the arsenal of solutions for his problem he said, "You Americans are stupid." The animals eating Manute's food—the ones he was trying to kill—were flies. All Chuck had to do was to buy some insect repellent and a fly swatter. There were moments like this every day. Manute was very proud and independent. After the first year he began to handle most of his own affairs.

David Letterman, Johnny Carson, GQ magazine, and other media outlets wanted to interview Manute. One moment Chuck was dealing with the heady world of primetime media and the next moment Chuck and Manute were playing roles in another episode of the *Twilight Zone*. Chuck's car was a hand-me-down 1962 Ford Falcon. They rigged the car so that Manute could sit in the back seat and Chuck would drive him anywhere he needed to go.

Manute had many fine qualities, but patience wasn't one of them. When Chuck was taking too long at the drycleaners or a convenience store, Manute would beep the car horn until Chuck came out with whatever he was tasked to do. After all, it was easy for Manute reach the horn from the back seat. Bob Ferry (Bullet's GM) was in the car the first time Manute practiced his driving skills at the old Capital Center parking lot in Landover. Chuck had said, "I'm not risking my life!" So it fell to Bob. The parking lot was huge, but there were parking lot lights strategically placed all over the lot and Manute had a few close calls. Bob got out of the car quite shaken and drained.

Manute loved to embellish the adventurous story about killing a lion with a spear in the Sudanese bush. The lion had eaten some of his cows and he knew what he had to do. Only a few people really knew that he waited until the lion was asleep before thrusting it through with his spear. "I'm not a crazy American. Who would want to kill a lion while it was awake?" he said. Awake. Asleep. This still adds up to quite a feat.

Manute endeared himself to the players, the management and the fans. Manute was very confident in his size, had an excellent work ethic, loved his Sudanese heritage, and was enthusiastic about life. He enjoyed being around people who were honest and truthful. A man without guile. He loved to play jokes on his teammates and was the brunt of many practical jokes. He could give it and he could take it. Sometimes he would chase teammates like Jeff Ruland and Jeff Malone out of the locker room, throwing his sneakers at them. We probably will never know what deviously funny things they were doing that elicited such an explosive response.

According to published salary statistics, during his decade-long tenure as an NBA player, Manute earned almost $6 million. That's a lot of money by any standards. It has been said that he donated much of his NBA earnings to his native Sudan. In later years after the glow of the basketball court lights had dimmed and the regular source of income had dried up, Manute was caught between his personal needs and the needs of his own people back in Sudan. It was easy to determine that he was focused on the latter, which drove him to the boxing ring, the hockey rink, the horse track and other things that could be compared to the old circus freak shows. He was willing to do anything to raise the awareness of the plight of his people and also to raise money for his cause. A selfless humanitarian bearing gifts—a winsome smile and a hearty laugh. Motivated and even driven by a cause bigger than himself.

Manute's father, a Dinka tribal chief, picked a name for him at birth that literally means "*special blessing*." A prophetic declaration of sorts, depicting the impact Manute would have on millions of people. My mind goes back to a pre-game chapel meeting in 1987 when Manute had a personal encounter with Jesus of the Bible. I remember the look on his face when it all made sense to him and he became aware of his place in God's story. A moment in time that would impact and shape how he lived out his life in the years that followed.

Yes, Manute had his faults, but he is now in the stands and we are on the court. He is part of the "heavenly cloud of witnesses" (Heb. 12:1) cheering us on to finish well. Still engaging in a bit of trash talking, no doubt. The way Manute lived his life—pouring out to those who are in need and who have absolutely no way of repaying him for his generosity—is wisdom for those of us who are yet alive . . . struggling with our own issues. And it also gives us a glimpse into Manute's profound understanding of what Jesus had done for him some 2,000 years ago. The ultimate "*special blessing*."

About the Author:

Joel A. Freeman, Ph.D., professional speaker and corporate trainer. Serial entrepreneur. Prolific writer. Motivational consultant/mentor to pro athletes and CEOs. Off-key singer and extremely bad dancer. Veteran chaplain of the NBA Washington Bullets/Wizards ('79-'98). Co-author of the book and award-winning film, *Return To Glory: The Powerful Stirring of the Black Man* (view film trailer here)—www.ReturnToGlory.org

ISPA Organizational Members

*The following are **Organizational Members** of the ISPA. These organizations represent the very best in the sporting community, as they uphold the ideals set forth by the ISPA mission statement and principals of practice. For more information on ISPA Organizational Membership please visit www.theISPA.org.*

Associates in Nutrition Therapy (http://www.associatesinnutrition.com)

5237 Summerlin
Commons Blvd.
Fort Myers, Florida 33907
Phone: (239) 826-2021

ATI Physical Therapy (http://www.atipt.com)

790 Remington Rd
Bolingbrook, IL 60440
Phone: (630) 296-2222

DX Sports Performance (http://www.dxsportsperformance.com)

From Glory Days (http://www.fromglorydays.com)

P.O. Box 421
Farmington, MI 48332
Phone: (248) 594-1070

Impormex USA (http://www.impormexusa.com)

25 N. Hoyne
Chicago, Illinois 60612
Phone: (312) 287-8406

Noggin Power 2 (http://www.nogginpower2.com)

25 East Washington
Suite 1615
Chicago, IL 60602
Phone: (312) 920-9522

PRO Physical Therapy (http://www.propt.com)

211 Executive Drive
Suite 11 Newark, DE 19702
Phone: 877-776-7858

PSB Academy (http://www.psb-academy.edu.sg/)

2985 Jalan Bukit Merah
Singapore 159457
Phone: 6370 8368

Sports Nutrition 2GO (http://www.sn2g.com)

Sports Nutrition 2Go Main Office
6659 Liberty Court
Liberty Township, Ohio 45044
Phone: (513) 779-6444

Teens 2 Teams (http://www.teens2teams.com)

Team-Building Education, Inc.
5008 Evergreen Ct.
McKinney, TX 75070
Phone: (972) 369-1128

The Freeman Institute (http://www.freemaninstitute.com)

P.O. Box 305
Gambrills, Maryland, 21054-0305
Phone: (410) 729-4011

The Institute of Sports Psychology (http://www.tinssp.com)

3701 Kirby Dr Suite 713
Houston, TX 77098
Phone: (713) 522-2200

Tri-Masters (http://www.trimasters.org)

Sports Initiative Programs PO Box 172
1448 East 52nd Street
Chicago, IL 60615-4122
Phone: (773) 980-8084